Fostering

Connections

Fostering

Connections

Building Student Relationships That Transform Teaching And Learning

Steven Menduke

If you care about someone, and you got a little love in your heart, there ain't nothing you can't get through together.
Ted Lasso

Acknowledgments

To my incredible, strong, beautiful, and intelligent fellow educator wife and life partner Krystle, who believed in me when no one else did. *I learn from you everyday.*

Contents

The roles have changed, the locations have changed, the students and families have changed, but one thing has remained constant: when there has been any level of success (academic, social, emotional, or cultural), it has been a result of authentic connection with others stemming from mutual understanding, respect, and love.

Introduction

Building meaningful relationships with students becomes a cornerstone of this anti-racist framework, facilitating a deeper understanding of individual experiences, cultures, and needs.

In the sun-kissed South Bay, a tranquil beach town just beyond the hustle and bustle of Los Angeles, my formative years unfolded against the backdrop of the Pacific Ocean. Nestled in a middle-class neighborhood, I was blissfully ignorant of the immense blessings that shaped my childhood and adolescence. Growing up in a two-parent home for most of my childhood and teenage years, and surrounded by a supportive community of friends and family, attending excellent schools was a privilege I accepted without much contemplation.

I spent most of my time at school doing just enough to get by without being noticed too much by adults on campus, and just enough to make sure my parents weren't too upset with me about my grades. The corridors of learning were familiar terrain, but the true value of education didn't register until I ventured beyond the sheltered cocoon of my upbringing. My academic journey became a solitary pursuit, devoid of the insights and perspectives that connections beyond textbooks and exams could have provided.

Beyond academics, my true passion lay in the world of baseball — a priority that defined my after-school hours. The sport not only provided a national platform for competition but also opened my eyes to the stark contrasts in backgrounds among my teammates, particularly along racial lines. Traveling for tournaments and games exposed me to a diversity of experiences that I had never seen before, prompting a deeper reflection on the disparities existing even among my local friends. This realization sparked a curiosity about diverse cultures and, over the following decade, led to a profound engagement with concepts of race, racism, and the dynamics of white supremacy and privilege.

Despite my lack of strong religious affiliations, being part of a Jewish family exposed me to a different form of discrimination. Insensitive jokes and encounters with bias served as poignant reminders of the challenges faced by others. However, my white-passing privilege shielded me from the full impact of discrimination, a realization that dawned on me as I transitioned from my baseball career to a role in education.

As an instructional aide in schools, questions about my impact on others, mindfulness toward diverse lived experiences, and the dynamics of relationships became central to my reflections. Wrestling with these questions has been an ongoing journey, shaping much of my life since then. *What is my role in the lives of those around me? How do I navigate relationships with mindfulness and respect for diverse experiences?* These questions have become guiding principles in my pursuit of understanding and empathizing with others in order to make a positive impact in the realm of education.

Over the last ten years, I have dedicated my life to learning, growing, and serving alongside students and families on school campuses in South Los Angeles and Denver. The roles have changed, the locations have changed, the students and families have changed, but one thing has remained constant: when there has been any level of success (academic, social, emotional, or cultural), it has been a result of authentic connection with others stemming from mutual understanding, respect, and love. Whether a teacher, an aide, a coach, a dean, or a principal, I am of the deep belief that the only way to be successful in education is by building, fostering, and maintaining relationships with young people. The question has always been, though (to quote Gloria Ladson-Billings), "Yes, But How Do We Do It?".

A Lightning Quick Guide for Educators

As I contemplate the educational landscape, a compelling truth surfaces—an urgent call for a paradigm shift in how we approach student engagement and success. The prevailing discourse often revolves around academic outcomes, standardized testing, and curriculum development, sidelining a crucial element for meaningful learning: *the relationships between educators and students.* This brief book emerges as a possible response to this critical gap, an earnest endeavor to redirect the narrative toward a more holistic understanding of education—one that recognizes the profound impact of genuine connections in shaping a student's academic and emotional journey.

While academic achievement undeniably stands as a cornerstone of educational success, the oversight of the relational dimension within schools is a significant flaw. Substantial research attests to the transformative power of positive teacher-student relationships, transcending the boundaries of traditional instruction to create an environment where students feel seen, heard, and valued. In a world inundated with data-driven metrics, it is crucial to acknowledge that a student's success extends beyond mere test scores, and, in many cases, the age-old adage of "students don't learn from people they don't like" holds true. This book serves as a call to educators, administrators, and policymakers to reassess priorities, placing the cultivation of meaningful relationships at the forefront of educational practices.

Undoubtedly, schools, especially those existing in underserved communities, face multifaceted challenges—resource disparities, systemic inequities, and the ever-evolving landscape of societal expectations. In the face of these complexities, the significance of positive relationships becomes even more pronounced. Students confronting adversity often bear external pressures, and a supportive relationship with an educator can act as an anchor, a source of inspiration, and a catalyst for resilience. This book aims to illuminate the potential for transformation inherent in these connections, providing a roadmap for educators navigating the challenges of serving students who, for generations, have been failed.

Addressing systemic issues ingrained in the education system demands an intentional and multifaceted approach. Central to this approach is the adoption of an anti-racist lens that permeates every aspect of the educational journey. Building meaningful relationships with students becomes a cornerstone of this anti-racist framework, facilitating a deeper understanding of individual experiences, cultures, and needs. Through these connections, educators can actively contribute to dismantling oppressive structures, fostering an inclusive environment where every student has the opportunity to thrive.

Recognizing the demanding nature of the teaching profession, this concise guide has been crafted with utmost consideration for the invaluable time teachers invest in shaping the future. *Fostering Connections: Building Student Relationships that Transform Teaching & Learning* is intentionally brief, offering a focused and action-oriented approach to empower educators with practical tools. My hope is that you will leverage this book as a quick read (we all know an educator's time is deeply impacted), providing immediate and impactful ways to enhance both your teaching practice and the educational journey of your students. This book is not just a read for reading's sake; instead, it is intended to be a swift and effective resource designed for the dynamic realities of the teaching profession.

Chapter 1: Understanding the Landscape

Breaking free from the self-fulfilling prophecy demands a concerted effort to disrupt these negative narratives.

Addressing the needs of underserved communities is a commendable yet intricate endeavor, marked by challenges that demand a keen understanding of the nuanced requirements of the students and families involved. Economic disparities, limited access to resources, and a history of systemic neglect present formidable obstacles for educators to navigate. The impact of systemic issues on education in underserved communities is a pervasive force that requires thorough examination. Historical inequities, discriminatory policies, and socioeconomic disparities contribute to an educational landscape where opportunities are not equitably distributed. The consequences of these disparities echo through generations, perpetuating cycles of disadvantage.

However, within these challenges also lie opportunities for transformative change. Adopting an anti-racist, trauma-informed approach becomes crucial in dismantling systemic barriers, opening the door to a more just and inclusive educational system. Recognizing the resilience and untapped potential within these communities, and more importantly, assisting young individuals in these communities to recognize their own brilliance, educators can cultivate a sense of empowerment and establish pathways for both academic and personal success. This shift in perspective acknowledges the inherent strength of underserved communities and seeks to break the cycles of disadvantage by providing tailored support and fostering a culture of inclusivity and empowerment within the educational framework.

The Self-Fulfilling Prophecy

The weight of low expectations becomes a generational burden for many students in underserved communities. When societal, educational, and self-imposed beliefs converge to reinforce the idea that academic success is unattainable, a self-fulfilling prophecy takes root. This detrimental cycle begins with setbacks exacerbated by a lack of resources, limited opportunities, and systemic neglect. As students encounter these obstacles, the prophecy gains strength, shaping their perception of their own capabilities and potential. Internalized limitations manifest in statements like, "I'm not good at math, so there's no point in trying," perpetuating a narrative that hinders their pursuit of academic achievement.

The self-fulfilling prophecy acts as a formidable barrier, as students internalize negative stereotypes and low expectations. This internalization influences their behavior, self-esteem, and approach to learning. Educators, consciously or unconsciously, may also contribute to lowered expectations, unintentionally fostering an environment where students are set up for failure rather than success.

Breaking free from the self-fulfilling prophecy demands a concerted effort to disrupt these negative narratives. Educators and leaders must challenge stereotypes, creating an environment that nurtures a growth mindset. Recognizing and celebrating small victories become pivotal in dismantling the self-fulfilling prophecy, instilling a sense of agency and cultivating resilience.

Systemic issues play a pivotal role in the complex landscape of underserved communities, casting a long and formidable shadow that shapes the experiences and opportunities of generations. Rooted in historical inequities, systemic issues perpetuate a cycle of disadvantage that profoundly influences the educational journey of students in these communities.

Understanding the historical context is crucial to comprehending the enduring impact of systemic issues. Discriminatory policies and systemic neglect have left lasting disparities that transcend generations. From unequal resource distribution to discriminatory practices, historical inequities permeate every facet of the educational experience. These disparities affect students navigating an educational landscape riddled with barriers.

Systemic issues manifest in glaring disparities in material and educational resources in underserved schools—insufficient funding, outdated facilities, and a lack of extracurricular opportunities. These deficiencies contribute to an uneven playing field, limiting educational experiences and influencing career choices, access to higher education, and life trajectories.

Challenges related to teacher quality and retention in underserved communities further exemplify systemic issues. Attracting and retaining experienced educators is a struggle, disrupting continuity and depriving students of crucial mentorship. This turnover contributes to a cycle of inconsistency, hindering student success.

The reliance on standardized testing exacerbates challenges faced by underserved communities. The emphasis on high-stakes testing narrows curricula, limiting exposure to a broad educational experience. This myopic approach disproportionately affects those without access to supplementary resources or test preparation.

In essence, systemic issues create a vicious cycle of disadvantage, affecting the educational journey of students in underserved communities. Historical inequities, resource disparities, teacher quality challenges, and standardized testing practices form a complex web of obstacles. Recognizing and addressing these issues is crucial for fostering true educational equity and breaking generational cycles of disadvantage.

Chapter 2:
Foundations of
Transformative
Relationships

Empathetic educators empower students to take ownership of their educational journey by respecting their voices, perspectives, and aspirations.

In the face of persistent systemic neglect in underserved communities, the profound impact of meaningful relationships between teachers and students emerges as a beacon of hope. These relationships, built on trust, empathy, and genuine care, play a pivotal role in dismantling the chains of systemic negligence and fostering equitable educational experiences.

Teacher-student relationships serve as a powerful counterforce to the effects of systemic neglect. In environments where resources are scarce and opportunities limited, the interpersonal connection between educators and students becomes a catalyst for resilience. A supportive relationship can counteract the negative impact of systemic issues, providing students with a sense of belonging and the belief that their potential is not constrained by their circumstances.

The importance of teacher-student relationships lies in their role in fostering a growth mindset. In the face of systemic challenges that may perpetuate a fixed mindset—where students believe their abilities are predetermined and unchangeable—positive relationships with teachers can instill the belief that effort, perseverance, and learning from setbacks lead to growth. This shift in mindset becomes a powerful tool in dismantling the self-fulfilling prophecies ingrained by systemic negligence.

Systemic policies often fail to address the diverse needs of students in underserved communities. Teacher-student relationships offer a remedy to this deficiency by providing individualized support and mentorship. Understanding the unique strengths, challenges, and aspirations of each student allows educators to tailor their approach, creating a learning environment that nurtures the specific needs of the individuals within it.

Beyond academic support, teacher-student relationships become a source of resilience and empowerment. In an educational landscape marked by systemic disparities, students encounter numerous obstacles. A supportive relationship with a teacher serves as a lifeline during these challenges, instilling resilience and empowering students to navigate the complexities of their educational journey. When students feel seen, heard, and valued, they are more likely to overcome systemic barriers and chart a path toward success.

The importance of teacher-student relationships in breaking the chain of systemic negligence cannot be overstated. These relationships not only counteract the negative effects of systemic challenges but also foster a growth mindset, provide individualized support, and cultivate resilience and empowerment. As catalysts for transformative change, positive teacher-student relationships stand as a cornerstone of educational equity, offering a pathway for students in underserved communities to transcend the limitations imposed by systemic neglect and shape their own destinies.

Relationships Built on Empathy, Not Sympathy

Empathy and cultural competence emerge as essential cornerstones towards cultivating genuine relationships between educators and students in underserved communities. These qualities not only lay the foundation for authentic connections but also act as antidotes to harmful dynamics like white saviorship. A commitment to empathy and cultural competence is crucial in creating an environment where students are active participants in their own growth and learning, rather than mere recipients of assistance.

Empathy, fundamentally, involves a profound understanding of the lived experiences of students. In underserved communities, where students grapple with challenges stemming from systemic neglect, poverty, or discrimination, empathetic educators seek to comprehend the multifaceted dimensions of these experiences. By acknowledging the uniqueness of each student's journey, educators can establish connections that transcend stereotypes and preconceived notions.

Cultural competence complements empathy, providing educators with a framework for respectful and inclusive interaction. It entails a commitment to understanding the cultural backgrounds, traditions, and values that shape the identities of students. A culturally competent educator recognizes the diversity within their classroom and leverages this understanding to create an environment where every student feels seen and valued.

Authentic relationships require vigilance against harmful dynamics like white saviorship, where the educator positions themselves as the savior of their students.

Empathy and cultural competence counteract these imbalances by promoting shared understanding and collaboration. Rather than imposing solutions, empathetic educators work alongside students and their communities, acknowledging that expertise and agency lie within the community itself.

The intersection of empathy and cultural competence fosters an environment where students are not passive recipients of assistance but active agents in their own growth and learning. Empathetic educators empower students to take ownership of their educational journey by respecting their voices, perspectives, and aspirations. This approach challenges traditional power dynamics, creating a space where students feel valued, heard, and equipped to shape their own destinies.

The role of empathy and cultural competence extends beyond interactions with students; it cultivates a growth mindset in educators themselves. The commitment to continuous learning and self-reflection enables educators to adapt their approaches, learn from their mistakes, and refine their cultural competence. In this way, empathy and cultural competence become not just tools for student growth but transformative forces shaping the entire educational ecosystem.

The authentic connections forged through empathy and cultural competence are paramount in nurturing student growth. By understanding and respecting the lived experiences of students, educators can dismantle harmful dynamics, guard against saviorship, and foster an environment where students are active participants in their educational journey. In embracing these principles, educators pave the way for a truly inclusive and empowering educational experience in underserved communities.

A Rising Tide...

The interconnection between student-teacher relationships and academic success is a linchpin that holds the potential to redefine educational outcomes. Research consistently highlights that the quality of relationships between educators and students is a key determinant of academic success, particularly in communities grappling with historical systemic challenges.

Student-teacher relationships serve as a framework for personalized support tailored to the unique needs and strengths of students in underserved communities. In an educational landscape often characterized by large class sizes and limited resources, the one-on-one connection fosters an environment where educators can identify specific areas of growth and provide targeted assistance. This personalized support is instrumental in addressing learning gaps, building foundational skills, and ensuring that students receive the attention necessary for academic success.

Steeped in trust and mentorship, student-teacher relationships become a navigational guide through challenges. Educators who understand the complexities of their students' lives can offer guidance, resources, and encouragement, serving as mentors who help students overcome obstacles both inside and outside the classroom. This mentorship extends beyond academics, influencing the development of crucial life skills and mindsets that contribute to overall success. In underserved communities, where limited opportunities and systemic neglect pose challenges, fostering a growth mindset becomes paramount. Positive relationships with educators, rooted in encouragement and belief in students' potential and genius, contribute to the cultivation of resilience. Students who feel supported are more likely to approach challenges with a belief in their ability to learn and grow, transcending the barriers imposed by systemic issues.

In communities burdened by low expectations, student-teacher relationships become a forceful countermeasure to self-fulfilling prophecies that can hinder academic success. When educators convey high expectations, provide unwavering support, and believe in the capabilities of their students, they disrupt the cycle of negative expectations ingrained by decades of neglect. The power of positive relationships lies in their ability to reshape narratives, instilling a sense of agency and possibility in students who may have been conditioned to believe in their limitations.

Student-teacher relationships significantly contribute to fostering a sense of belonging and purpose among young people. Students who feel connected to their educators and their school environment are more likely to actively engage in the learning process. The age-old saying, "Kids don't learn from teachers they don't like," rings mostly true here. This sense of belonging serves as a motivational force, propelling students to strive for academic success not only for individual achievement but also for the betterment of their own community.

The nexus between student-teacher relationships and academic success in underserved communities is a potent force for transformative change. These relationships provide the scaffolding for personalized support, mentorship through systemic challenges, cultivation of a growth mindset, disruption of negative prophecies, and the creation of a nurturing environment that fosters academic achievement. As educators and students forge these meaningful connections, they unlock the potential for success that transcends the limitations imposed by systemic inequities.

Chapter 3:
Restorative Practices and Community Building

Central to restorative practices is the emphasis on open and honest dialogue.

Restorative practices in schools mark a paradigm shift in the approach to discipline and community-building. Rooted in principles of accountability, empathy, and repairing harm, these practices prioritize relationships and the well-being of the entire school community. This transformative approach seeks not only to address conflicts but also to build a culture of understanding, responsibility, and shared values.

At its core, restorative practices are founded on the belief that when harm occurs in a community, the focus should be on repairing the harm rather than solely punishing the wrongdoer. This approach recognizes the interconnectedness of individuals within a community and aims to strengthen the bonds that tie them together. Restorative practices draw inspiration from indigenous and traditional community-based justice models, emphasizing dialogue, understanding, and collective responsibility, while de-emphasizing hierarchy and power dynamics.

Central to restorative practices is the emphasis on open and honest dialogue. When conflicts arise, restorative processes involve bringing together those affected, including the wrongdoer and the harmed party, in a facilitated conversation. This dialogue provides an opportunity for individuals to share their perspectives, express their feelings, and collaboratively work towards a resolution. The focus is on active listening, empathy, and fostering a sense of connection among community members. Unlike punitive approaches that often perpetuate a cycle of resentment, restorative practices seek to repair harm and rebuild relationships. This may involve concrete actions aimed at making amends, acknowledging the impact of one's actions, and actively working towards rebuilding trust. Through this restorative lens, discipline becomes an opportunity for learning and growth rather than a punitive measure, contributing to a positive and supportive school climate fueled by authentic relationships built on mutual accountability.

Implementing restorative practices extends beyond addressing individual incidents; it involves cultivating a restorative school culture. This encompasses embedding restorative principles into everyday interactions, classroom dynamics, and decision-making processes. Restorative practices become a way of life within the school community, shaping the overall ethos and contributing to a sense of collective responsibility for the well-being of all members.

One of the key benefits of restorative practices is the empowerment of students. By involving them in the resolution process and fostering a sense of agency, restorative practices equip students with valuable conflict resolution and communication skills. Additionally, restorative approaches strengthen the sense of community within the school, fostering a supportive environment where individuals feel heard, understood, and valued regardless of their "position" within the community. Restorative practices in schools represent a holistic and transformative approach to discipline and community-building. By prioritizing dialogue, repairing harm, and fostering a restorative school culture, this approach not only addresses conflicts but also contributes to the development of responsible, empathetic, and empowered individuals within a thriving school community.

Restorative Practices in Action

In the realm of school settings, a tangible application of restorative practices comes to life through the utilization of restorative circles in the classroom. These circles offer a structured and deliberate space for both students and teachers to partake in open dialogue, exchange experiences, and establish connections. Proactively, circles can be employed to construct a positive classroom culture, emphasizing weekly discussions on uplifting experiences or shared values to nurture a sense of community. Reactively, circles can convene to address specific incidents, allowing individuals involved to articulate their feelings, comprehend diverse perspectives, and collaboratively devise a path forward, effectively restoring any harm caused.

Another instrumental tool for conflict resolution within a school context is the implementation of restorative conferencing. When conflicts arise, whether between students or involving students and staff, a restorative conference brings all parties to the table. Guided by a skilled mediator, this conference provides a structured platform for individuals to share experiences, express emotions, and collectively work towards resolution. The focus is not on assigning blame but on comprehending the impact of actions and collaboratively deciding on reparative measures. This process instills a sense of responsibility, fosters empathy, and contributes to rebuilding relationships within the school community.

In addition, schools can infuse restorative practices into community-building events to fortify connections among students, staff, and families. For instance, organizing a restorative justice assembly provides a platform for the school community to discuss shared values, celebrate accomplishments, and address concerns collectively. Furthermore, restorative practices can seamlessly integrate into traditional events such as parent-teacher conferences, transforming them into collaborative conversations centered around the student's well-being and development. By weaving restorative principles into various school activities, a culture of understanding, accountability, and connection takes root, fostering a positive and inclusive learning environment.

Respecting Diversity and Cultural Norms

In recognizing the manifold advantages that restorative practices bring to families, it becomes imperative to acknowledge and honor the diversity embedded in family structures, values, and communication styles. Underserved communities, often characterized by a tapestry of cultural backgrounds, encompass individuals who navigate parenting and conflict resolution through distinct lenses. The implementation of restorative practices in schools demands a nuanced approach that embraces this diversity, understanding that what proves effective for one family may markedly differ for another.

Within this landscape, schools assume a supportive role, introducing restorative practices as options rather than imperatives. Acknowledging the varied dynamics and communication styles within families, schools act as facilitators, equipping families with tools and resources to explore and integrate restorative practices into their unique contexts. This approach respects the autonomy of families, allowing them to naturally adopt restorative practices in alignment with their existing values and traditions.

Central to this process is the establishment of trust between schools and families, a foundation crucial for the successful integration of restorative practices. Schools approach families with humility, recognizing that they are the experts in their own experiences. Embracing a collective approach, schools create spaces for shared learning, where families draw from each other's strengths and cultural practices, enriching the overall understanding and application of restorative principles. By fostering collaborative learning environments, schools empower families to adapt restorative practices in ways that authentically resonate with their individual circumstances.

The introduction of restorative practices should be viewed by schools as an invitation for families to explore new possibilities rather than a mandate to conform. By respecting the diversity of family practices, acknowledging cultural variations, providing options instead of mandates, fostering collaborative learning, and building trust, schools can seamlessly integrate restorative practices into the fabric of family life. This collaborative approach establishes a harmonious partnership for the benefit of students and the entire community.

Chapter 4:
Strategies to Combat Trauma in our Communities

Underserved communities have grappled with the enduring consequences of economic strain over the last decade.

Over the past decade, underserved communities have faced an alarming prevalence of trauma, creating profound challenges that ripple through the fabric of daily life. From systemic inequalities to economic hardships and the compounding effects of global crises, individuals in these communities have borne the weight of adversity, shaping their experiences in profound ways. Underserved communities have grappled with the enduring consequences of economic strain over the last decade. The fallout from the 2008 financial crisis, coupled with ongoing disparities in employment opportunities and wage gaps, has created a persistent cycle of financial instability for many families. Economic hardships contribute to heightened stress levels, impacting mental and emotional well-being and leaving lasting imprints on the community's collective psyche. At the same time, there has been a heightened awareness of systemic inequalities, particularly in relation to racial injustice. While the focus has yielded much needed and long overdue shifts in mindsets, legislation, and action across the globe, underserved communities, often predominantly composed of people of color, have borne the brunt of these inequities and the fallout from these shifts. The trauma of racial injustice, both systemic and explicit, has left an indelible mark on individuals within these communities, exacerbating existing challenges and shaping the lens through which they navigate the world. More recently, the prevalence of health crises, notably the ongoing global pandemic, has introduced a new layer of trauma into underserved communities. Limited access to healthcare resources, higher susceptibility to health risks, and the disproportionate impact of the pandemic on these communities have contributed to a sense of collective trauma. Families have faced the loss of loved ones, economic instability, and the overarching uncertainty that accompanies health crises, amplifying the challenges they already endure.

Through this all, underserved communities have experienced significant disruptions in education and learning. From inadequate access to technology for remote learning to the challenges of navigating a system that often falls short in addressing diverse learning needs, students in these communities have encountered barriers to educational success that young folks in other communities took on with far more resources and support. These disruptions not only impede academic progress but also contribute to a form of learning trauma, where students may develop negative associations with education and face long-term consequences in their academic journey.

Now, as students have returned to school full time, it is imperative that we build, deconstruct and rebuild as many times as it takes, school communities centered around genuine and authentic relationships between adults and young people.

Some Strategies

Building relationships with young people stems from knowing yourself well enough to be authentic and vulnerable with the folks sitting across from you. In other words, be yourself. Among the many tools that students have at their disposal today, one of them is a keen ability to detect, for lack of a better term, bullshit. Acknowledging the diversity of experiences, backgrounds, and aspirations on any given campus, and how they are similar and different from my own, allows me to approach each student as an individual with distinct needs and strengths. Even better, knowing who I am allows me to commit to that approach in a way that is authentic, easy-going, welcoming, and, most importantly, honest. This perspective informs my interactions, ensuring that my approach to building relationships is not one-size-fits-all but rather a nuanced and responsive endeavor that also lets students know that the adult sitting across from them is a human being, also on their own journey.

Get Out There

In the bustling rhythm of school life, the importance of venturing beyond the classroom walls and embracing outdoor engagement with students cannot be overstated. Stepping into the open air, whether during lunch breaks, nutrition times, or at various school events, fosters a dynamic and holistic approach to building relationships. This intentional embrace of outdoor spaces goes beyond the confines of traditional academic settings, creating opportunities for genuine connections to flourish.

Leaving the formal structure of the classroom behind opens the door to informal bonds and shared experiences. The outdoor environment provides a relaxed setting where conversations can unfold organically, unburdened by the formalities of lesson plans. Whether it's a casual stroll across the campus, a picnic on the school grounds, or a moment of connection under the open sky, these outdoor encounters contribute to the development of relationships based on authenticity and shared moments. The informality of outdoor interactions can dissolve perceived hierarchies, creating a level playing field where students and educators engage as individuals rather than roles. This leveling effect fosters a sense of camaraderie, allowing students to see their educators not just as authority figures but as companions in the shared journey of learning.

Attending sporting events, dances, performances, and other extracurricular activities further strengthens the fabric of student-teacher relationships. Sharing in the excitement of these events demonstrates a commitment to understanding and participating in the broader aspects of students' lives. Whether cheering at a football game, applauding a musical performance, or celebrating achievements at a dance, these shared experiences create lasting memories and contribute to a sense of community within the school. It also sends a powerful message that educators are not only invested in academic success but also in the overall well-being and happiness of their students. This sense of belonging is foundational to building a positive and supportive school culture where students feel valued not just for their academic achievements but as unique individuals with diverse interests and talents.

The intentional embrace of outdoor engagement is a dynamic strategy in the toolkit of relationship-building between educators and students. Beyond the confines of the classroom, these outdoor interactions offer avenues for informal connections, breaking down barriers, sharing in the excitement of events, nurturing a sense of belonging, and strengthening social-emotional bonds. By weaving these outdoor moments into the fabric of school life, educators lay the groundwork for relationships that extend beyond the academic realm, fostering a supportive and vibrant community within the educational landscape.

Be Curious, Not Judgmental

In the intricate dance of student interactions, adopting a stance of curiosity over judgment proves to be a transformative and empowering approach. This mindset shift transcends the boundaries of traditional teacher-student dynamics, fostering a culture where understanding takes precedence over assumptions. Whether facing disciplinary issues, hearing stories about students' lives outside school, or encountering moments of vulnerability like a student with their head down on a desk, the call to be curious becomes a guiding principle for building authentic connections.

When faced with disciplinary challenges, the reflexive response may lean towards judgment or assumption. However, embracing curiosity opens the door to a deeper understanding of the root causes behind behavior. Instead of jumping to conclusions, educators can inquire about the factors influencing a student's actions, seeking to uncover the motivations and circumstances that may be contributing to the behavior. This curiosity-driven approach transforms disciplinary moments into opportunities for empathy, connection, and proactive problem-solving. For instance, encountering a student with their head down on a desk is a moment of vulnerability that calls for curiosity over judgment. Rather than assuming laziness or disinterest, educators can approach such situations with compassionate curiosity. By inquiring about the student's well-being, understanding potential stressors, or offering a supportive conversation, educators create an atmosphere where vulnerability is met with empathy. This curiosity-driven response transforms moments of vulnerability into opportunities for connection and support.

It is imperative to center our actions around the acknowledgement that every student carries a narrative that extends far beyond the confines of the classroom. Instead of making assumptions based on appearances or preconceived notions, curiosity invites educators to actively seek out the stories that shape students' lives. By engaging in open and non-judgmental conversations, educators gain insights into the challenges, triumphs, and aspirations that define students' experiences outside school. This curiosity-driven connection goes beyond the surface, fostering a genuine understanding that forms the foundation of a supportive and inclusive learning environment. Instead of shutting down or reacting with judgment, educators can cultivate a curiosity-driven dialogue that encourages students to share their perspectives and feelings. This open communication is a two-way street, allowing educators to convey genuine interest in students' experiences and, in turn, fostering an environment where students feel comfortable expressing their thoughts, concerns, and aspirations.

In the realm of student interactions, the choice to be curious instead of judgmental builds bridges of understanding rather than walls of misconception. It signals to students that their educators are invested in knowing them as individuals, beyond the surface impressions. This curiosity-driven approach contributes to the creation of a trusting and respectful relationship, where students feel acknowledged and valued. As educators embrace curiosity, they unlock the potential for transformative connections that transcend the traditional roles of teacher and student. It is an acknowledgment that each student is a unique individual with a story, experiences, and challenges that shape their journey, just as their teacher is. This mindset shift not only enriches the educational experience but also lays the groundwork for meaningful relationships that endure beyond the classroom.

The Power of an Unflinching Belief

Holding high expectations stands as a powerful expression of belief in students' potential. Rigor becomes the key ingredient, signaling to students that they are capable of achieving more than they may have thought possible. This approach transcends antiquated traditional notions of setting low bars for certain students; instead, it embraces a philosophy of pushing individuals to rise to their fullest capacities, and loving them at each step along the way.

This belief in students communicates the conviction that every individual has the capacity for excellence and growth, regardless and in spite of circumstance. By establishing challenging academic standards, educators send a clear message that they see and value the untapped potential within each student. This belief-driven approach lays the foundation for a transformative educational experience, where students are inspired to stretch beyond their perceived limits. Rigor, when infused into the learning environment, has a transformative impact on student outcomes. It challenges students to engage deeply with the material, fostering critical thinking, problem-solving skills, and a resilient attitude toward challenges. High expectations create a culture where success is not measured by meeting minimal requirements but by striving for mastery and continuous improvement. This rigorous standard-setting becomes a catalyst for self-discovery, instilling in students the confidence to tackle complex tasks and navigate academic hurdles.

Central to the philosophy of high expectations is the concept of radical candor—a balance between honesty and empathy in providing feedback. Radical candor, spoken about at length by Kim Scott in her text, *Radical Candor*, involves offering direct and honest feedback while maintaining a deep understanding of the individual's potential and aspirations. It is a departure from ruinous empathy, where feedback may be softened to avoid discomfort but ultimately hinders the growth of the individual. Radical candor fosters an environment where students receive genuine guidance and constructive criticism, leading to meaningful progress, not as punishment, but instead, as yet another showing of their teacher's belief in them.

Ultimately, high expectations, coupled with radical candor, become integral to the process of relationship-building with students. It signals to young people that educators are not merely content with mediocrity but are invested in their journey toward excellence. This shared commitment to rigorous standards creates a sense of partnership, where educators and students collaborate in the pursuit of academic and personal growth, for both parties. The relationships forged in this environment are built on mutual respect, trust, and a shared understanding of the transformative power of high expectations and support.

The philosophy of high expectations aligns seamlessly with nurturing a growth mindset—a belief that abilities and intelligence can be developed through dedication and hard work. By fostering a growth mindset, educators encourage students to embrace challenges, learn from setbacks, and persist in the face of difficulties. This mindset shift not only fuels academic success but also contributes to the development of resilience, curiosity, and a lifelong love for learning.

Building relationships with students through the lens of high expectations and rigor is a dynamic and belief-driven approach. It signifies a commitment to fostering transformative educational experiences, where students are empowered to reach for the stars and educators play a crucial role in guiding them on this journey. Through the delicate balance of radical candor and high expectations, educators create a learning environment where relationships are grounded in the shared pursuit of excellence and the unwavering belief in the limitless potential of every student.

Make it Clear

While educators are not positioned to be students' friends, the delicate balance of support and accountability is pivotal in fostering an environment of trust, respect, and growth. This nuanced approach involves being a steadfast ally who has their back, holds them accountable, believes in their potential, and guides them toward self-directed decision-making.

Being an ally to students involves providing unwavering support while maintaining a clear understanding of professional boundaries. This support extends beyond academic pursuits to encompass the challenges and triumphs students encounter in various facets of their lives. By conveying a genuine concern for their well-being, educators become trusted figures who offer a reliable foundation of support, creating an environment where students feel seen, heard, and valued.

Clear boundaries also include the expectation of accountability. While educators believe in students' potential, holding them accountable for their actions and decisions is a crucial aspect of the relationship. Accountability fosters a sense of responsibility and ownership, essential attributes for personal and academic growth. By setting clear expectations and consequences, educators provide a structured framework that guides students toward making informed choices and understanding the impact of their decisions.

Educators are not in the role of directing students toward specific paths; rather, they serve as guides in the journey of self-discovery. Clear boundaries demarcate the parameters within which students can explore, learn, and make decisions autonomously. This approach encourages the development of critical thinking skills, self-reflection, and the ability to navigate complex choices, laying the groundwork for a future where students are equipped to make informed decisions independently. The essence of clear boundaries lies in building skills, not fostering dependency. As educators provide the necessary support and accountability, they simultaneously equip students with the skills to navigate challenges, solve problems, and make choices aligned with their values (or even identify their values at all). This skill-building approach is a long-term investment in the students' capacity to navigate the complexities of life beyond the classroom, instilling in them a sense of agency and self-efficacy.

As educators play the role of allies who believe in students' potential, hold them accountable, and guide them toward autonomous decision-making, they create an environment where relationships are grounded in trust, respect, and a shared commitment to growth. Through this intentional approach, educators contribute not only to academic success but also to the fostering of resilient, responsible, and empowered individuals prepared for the challenges and opportunities that may lie ahead.

The Cs

Finally, two steadfast pillars emerge as indispensable for student success: consistency and continuity. Students flourish when they are provided with a stable and predictable environment, where expectations are clear, and communication is consistent. Being a reliable and unwavering force in a student's life holds immeasurable importance, contributing to a sense of security, trust, and the optimal conditions for academic and personal growth.

Consistency in setting clear expectations forms the bedrock of a student's sense of security within the educational landscape. When students know what is expected of them, academically and behaviorally, it creates a stable foundation upon which they can build their educational journey. This clarity reduces uncertainty and anxiety, allowing students to focus on learning and personal development rather than navigating unpredictable expectations. Along with this, continuity in communication is a cornerstone of building trust and rapport with students. A consistent flow of information, updates, and feedback establishes a reliable channel for students to understand their progress, address concerns, and celebrate achievements. This continuity in communication goes beyond the academic realm, encompassing a holistic approach that recognizes and supports students' overall well-being.

Consistency in the learning environment enhances stability, creating an atmosphere conducive to academic success. From instructional methods to classroom routines, students benefit from a sense of predictability. This stability allows them to focus on the content and skills being taught, maximizing their engagement and participation in the learning process. A consistent and stable learning environment is particularly crucial for students facing external challenges, as it provides a reliable anchor amid potential turmoil. Being a consistent force in a student's life is instrumental in building meaningful relationships. Students thrive when they can rely on educators to be present, engaged, and supportive consistently. This reliability fosters a sense of connection and trust, essential components for creating a positive and nurturing educational experience. Building relationships based on consistency opens the door for open communication, mutual understanding, and a shared commitment to growth.

The impact of consistency and continuity extends far beyond the immediate academic context; it lays the groundwork for long-term student development. When educators consistently provide a stable and supportive environment, students are more likely to develop resilience, self-efficacy, and a positive attitude toward learning. These qualities, cultivated through years of reliable guidance, become integral aspects of a student's character, influencing their approach to challenges and opportunities beyond the educational setting. The importance of consistency and continuity in education cannot be overstated. These pillars contribute significantly to the overall well-being and success of students, creating an environment where they can thrive academically, emotionally, and socially. By fostering clear expectations, predictable communication, stability in learning environments, and reliable relationships, educators become architects of a foundation that supports students not just in their academic pursuits but in their journey toward becoming empowered and resilient individuals ready to face the complexities of their present and the future.

Focus on the Good

In the pursuit of fostering student development, the lens through which educators view their students becomes a defining factor. An asset-based approach, centered on recognizing and leveraging students' inherent strengths and capabilities, stands as a transformative paradigm. This perspective shifts the narrative from deficits and challenges to a celebration of the unique assets each student brings to the learning environment. Embracing an asset-based philosophy not only bolsters students' self-esteem but also lays the groundwork for a holistic and empowering educational experience.

An asset-based approach begins with the fundamental recognition that every student possesses a wealth of unique assets, talents, and perspectives. By acknowledging and

33

valuing these inherent qualities, educators set the stage for unleashing the full potential within each student. Highlighting students' strengths nurtures a profound sense of confidence and self-efficacy. When students see their capabilities acknowledged and celebrated, they are more inclined to take risks, embrace challenges, and engage actively in their own learning journey. An asset-based approach empowers students to see themselves as contributors to the learning process, instilling in them a belief in their ability to overcome obstacles and achieve success.

Traditional deficit-based models often focus on what students lack or struggle with, creating a narrative of shortcomings. An asset-based perspective, however, shifts the narrative to one of resilience. Instead of viewing challenges as insurmountable obstacles, educators see them as opportunities for growth and development. This shift in mindset promotes a culture of perseverance and tenacity, where setbacks are seen as integral steps on the path to success. Along with this, an asset-based approach inherently fosters a culture of inclusion and diversity. By recognizing and celebrating the diverse assets each student brings to the table, educators create an environment where differences are not only accepted but embraced. This inclusive culture contributes to a richer and more vibrant learning community, where students feel valued for their individual contributions and cultural backgrounds.

Embracing an asset-based philosophy contributes to holistic student development. It goes beyond academic achievements to encompass social, emotional, and interpersonal growth. Educators become partners in students' overall well-being, recognizing that the skills and strengths developed during their educational journey are invaluable assets for lifelong learning and success. By recognizing and celebrating the inherent assets within each student, educators not only nurture confidence and resilience but also foster a culture of inclusion and diversity. This approach lays the foundation for holistic student development, empowering individuals to navigate challenges, embrace opportunities, and cultivate a lifelong love for learning.

Chapter 5:
From the Voice of a
Student

The confidence to overcome struggles and the belief that setbacks were not insurmountable hurdles were instilled in me by the supportive relationships teachers built with me in high school.

Voices of students on our campuses weave a narrative that is as diverse and unique as the individuals themselves. This chapter delves into the invaluable perspective of one of my (recently) former students, illuminating the profound impact that teacher-student relationships have had on her educational journey. Acknowledging the essential role of student voice in understanding the dynamics of the classroom, we embark on a journey of reflection and revelation.

Student voice is not merely a reflection but a guiding force, steering the narrative towards a more inclusive and empathetic understanding of the educational landscape. As we explore the stories shared by students, we recognize the transformative power of genuine connections in the classroom and the lasting impressions left by educators who recognized the inherent value of each student's voice. This chapter serves as a testament to the importance of creating spaces where students are not just recipients of knowledge but active participants in their educational journey, contributing to a collective narrative that celebrates the myriad of ways teacher-student relationships shape the future.

There is no one better suited to speak to the importance, impact, and reality of student-teacher relationships than the students themselves. In crafting this guide towards helping teachers build transformative relationships with students, it was important for me to connect with students that I have been fortunate enough to know and work with. Enter the arena class of 2017 high school graduate, and class of 2021 college graduate, "Samantha" (name changed). Samantha is a young, Latina woman born and raised in East Los Angeles, California. She comes from a largely one parent household, and represents the first generation in her family to attend and graduate from both high school and university. I had the chance to connect with Samantha to hear about her journey through her secondary education, her experiences in college, and how each of those have shaped her life as a woman of color in the STEM field of environmental engineering.

Here is what she had to say:

Question: Reflecting on your educational journey, can you share a specific memory or experience where a teacher or educator had a positive impact on your life? What made this interaction memorable for you?

Samantha's Response: *In my personal life, not exclusively in the context of education, there's a vivid memory that stands out. I was a member of the soccer team, and during a particularly challenging time at home, it had a noticeable impact on my performance on the field.*

While I wasn't the star player, I also wasn't the weakest link. My coach recognized this and took the initiative to address the situation. He pulled me aside and expressed genuine concern, saying, "You don't need to tell me what's happening, but if something's affecting you, and you're not fully present, we can take a break for the day to collect yourself and come back."

This interaction made me realize that, with this coach, our relationship went beyond the conventional teacher-student dynamic. His understanding and support extended to my role as a player on the soccer team. He was also just generally caring for me and probably other students. And I think that helped me pay more attention on the field and in class.

Question: In your opinion, what qualities or characteristics do you believe make a teacher approachable and supportive? Can you recall a teacher who exemplified these qualities, and how did it influence your learning experience?

Samantha's Response: *The most impactful quality I've found in teachers, extending even through college, is empathy. This quality stands out as it transforms a teacher into a genuine person, especially during my college years.*

In college, the majority of my professors demonstrated empathy, making them more relatable. On the contrary, in school, a significant portion of the teachers seemed disinterested, following a routine of delivering lectures and leaving. If you had questions, the onus was on you to seek them out.

High school, however, presented a different scenario. Teachers actively engaged, asking questions, reaching out, and expressing genuine concern when they sensed a struggle. Their empathy made a significant impact, fostering an environment where it was clear that they cared about the students and their well-being inside and outside of school.

In college, I quickly learned that not all professors possessed this quality. Some seemed indifferent or lacked the empathy exhibited by my high school teachers. It became evident that the caring and empathetic approach might not universally apply to college settings, or perhaps it was specific to certain educators.

The standout quality for me is undeniably when a teacher or professor displays empathy toward students. Classes with empathetic professors proved to be far more enriching, and I performed significantly better compared to situations where the teacher showed little care and was solely focused on delivering content without regard for the students' well-being.

In the college setting, this straightforwardness reached a point where professors openly expressed their sole focus on teaching and leading, often emphasizing that their primary commitment was to research. Some professors were overt about their perspective, stating that students would only succeed if they cared enough, creating an environment where the course became more challenging.

I encountered two professors who, from the outset, declared that their courses were designed to be rigorous to filter out students. Unfortunately, I failed both of these classes initially. High school and middle school provided a slightly different experience, possibly influenced by my unique situation of attending charter schools throughout. In my memory, charter schools excelled at hiring teachers who genuinely cared. I struggle to recall an instance where a teacher didn't show care throughout my middle to high school career in the charter school system.

Question: Were there moments in your academic journey when you faced challenges or setbacks? How did teachers or educators contribute to your resilience and ability to overcome obstacles?

Samantha's Response: *When I was in college, I really struggled with this one math class, Calculus 2 to be exact. I actually failed that class twice, and it got to the point where my counselor let me know that if I did not pass this class on my third attempt, I would need to change my major.*

During each attempt to pass that class, I had a different professor. The first one had a system based on a curve, guaranteeing that about 40% of students would fail. While there was an opportunity to jump to an A if you performed exceptionally well, even a slight miss would result in a C or failure. I disliked this approach intensely. Worst of all, the professor didn't really spend any time getting to know students, or building any type of connection with us. The class and the experience itself felt cold and detached.

The second professor, while not bad, couldn't shake off the negative impact of my prior experience. The subject matter became triggering, hindering my ability to engage. So, really, by no fault of this professor, my whole view of this class was tainted by my first experience and lack of connection.

For the third attempt, I enrolled in a summer course with a different professor. This instructor took a hands-on approach, providing examples, demonstrating applications, and then having us solve problems independently in class. The small class size, capped at around 20 students, facilitated a more interactive environment. The professor dedicated time during lectures to address students' questions. The third time proved different. The professor was approachable and blunt, providing clear feedback on misunderstandings. They provided precise feedback, identified my challenges, and guided me on the necessary mindset shift. This unique approach led me to end the class with an A, achieving a 95%! I found it challenging to process this success considering the teaching methods of other educators. Trust played a crucial role for me; feedback was more impactful when it came from someone I trusted on some level. This professor broke down walls of trauma around this class and the lack of connection with other professors. Once those walls were down, I was ready for all of the feedback, and I thrived!

Question: How did building relationships with teachers impact you in life both in school and after school?

Samantha's Response: *The significance of school culture cannot be overstated, and really is all about how teachers connect with students. Reflecting on my brother's experience in a large school compared to my more intimate high school, the contrast was black and white. In his larger school, there was a sense of detachment, lacking the warmth and personal connection I cherished in my high school. Teachers in my high school went beyond merely instructing; they fostered individual relationships with each student, ensuring everyone reached their highest potential. This personalized approach was the driving force behind my commitment to education. Had I been in a less interactive environment, I might have treated classes as a routine, attending without genuine engagement.*

The interactive and caring nature of the teachers instilled a desire to actively participate in school activities, join the soccer team, attend after-school events, and excel in engineering classes. It created a sense of belonging and motivated me to contribute to the school's positive statistics, showcasing its dedication to students' success, regardless of background. Teachers really went above and beyond to show me that they not only wanted me to succeed in their class, but that they could learn from me too. For example, one teacher who came from a different cultural background than me and my peers would bring in food from their culture and try food from our cultures. Other teachers attended outside of school events like family quinceaneras, baptisms, etc. when invited. This really showed us that these people were not just there for our math or history classes, but they were there because they cared about us. They loved us.

When I left high school I felt well-prepared for college, maybe not as much academically, but more than enough socially and emotionally. The confidence to overcome struggles and the belief that setbacks were not insurmountable hurdles were instilled in me by the supportive relationships teachers built with me in high school. This emotional resilience became a cornerstone for navigating the difficulties encountered in college, and in life, really. It's not about comparing academic and social-emotional knowledge; both are crucial. But my teachers' contribution wasn't just about academic readiness but instead, cultivating a growth mindset, perseverance, and self-assurance. As I faced challenges in college, I carried this foundation, knowing I could weather the storm and emerge stronger.

This readiness to embrace challenges with a positive mindset is a testament to the holistic education I received, preparing me not just academically but socially and emotionally for the complexities of life beyond school.

Certainly, in high school, the relationships with teachers were invaluable. They not only taught me subject matter but also demonstrated the importance of recognizing mistakes and the value of setbacks. Learning that it's acceptable to take steps back as long as one moves forward significantly impacted my approach to academics and now in my professional career.

In the working world, there's no one holding my hand, especially in a remote work setting. The lessons from those teachers about self-reliance and resilience have proven crucial. The ability to embrace mistakes, learn from them, and continuously improve has been a guiding principle. This mindset transitioned seamlessly into my professional life, where I've experienced setbacks but have a boss who, like those teachers, encourages growth through constructive feedback. Her supportive approach, acknowledging that making mistakes is part of the learning process, mirrors the positive influence of my high school teachers. I'm fortunate to have such guidance, fostering trust in my professional journey.

Question: As a student, what advice would you give to educators about the importance of building meaningful relationships with their students? How can teachers create an environment that fosters trust, understanding, and academic success?

Samantha's Response: *The advice I would offer is to view each student as an individual. While considering overall class statistics is important, it's equally crucial to assess each student's progress individually. Whether a student is struggling or not, initiating one-on-one conversations can be beneficial. Engaging with students, asking for their thoughts on the class, and being open to suggestions for improvement fosters a supportive environment. Teachers, despite their qualifications, can also learn from their students. Every class has a unique mix of learning mindsets, and seeking feedback on what works and what doesn't can be insightful. Encouraging dialogue about potential changes or incorporating new approaches creates an inclusive and dynamic learning environment. This practice applies to both new and experienced teachers.*

Certainly, being open to feedback is crucial. Consider each student as your customer, valuing their perspective. Recognize that they are the most important individuals in the learning space. It's essential to evaluate whether your teaching methods are effective and, if not, find ways to make them work. Encourage open communication and be receptive to feedback. As a teacher, it's okay not to have all the right answers. Avoid adopting a rigid approach where it's "my way or no way." Flexibility and openness contribute to creating an environment that caters to diverse learning needs and fosters positive student-teacher relationships.

Along with this, it is important that teachers hold students accountable! We can see the teachers who want to just be "nice" to us. More often than not, kids will take advantage of those teachers. Instead, show us that you believe in us, and because of that belief, you are going to make sure we are doing what we need to do to grow in our studies, but also as young human beings. Accountability, to me, is love and care.

It is clear that the transformative impact of genuine teacher-student relationships extends far beyond the individual, radiating its influence throughout entire school communities. As Samantha shared her story, a common theme emerged: the profound ripple effect connections have on personal growth, academic success, and overall well-being. For many, these relationships serve as a cornerstone, a source of inspiration that not only shapes their educational experience but also fosters a sense of belonging and purpose. This transformative influence radiates outward, creating a positive atmosphere that permeates the school community.

The school community, like a tapestry woven from diverse threads, is strengthened by the bonds forged in these meaningful relationships. As students like Samantha experience personal growth, their newfound confidence and enthusiasm contribute to a positive and vibrant school culture. The impact extends to the broader network of educators, administrators, and support staff, creating a collective commitment to fostering an environment where every student feels seen, heard, and valued. The transformative nature of these relationships doesn't merely enhance the academic landscape; it cultivates a sense of unity and shared purpose that reverberates throughout the entire school community.

In essence student and teacher relationships are non-negotiable. They shape the culture, ethos, and collective identity of the school, creating an environment where empathy, understanding, and support are not just ideals but integral components of the educational journey. In this chapter, Samantha illuminates the profound influence of these relationships on both the individual and the broader school community, underscoring the essential role they play in helping students find success in school, yes, but even more importantly, in life.

Chapter 6:
Overcoming Resistance
and Skepticism

Position relationship-building not as a diversion but as a complementary and essential component for sustainable educational success.

Navigating the whirlwind of responsibilities as a young teacher, the commitment to relationship building might initially feel like an additional task on an overflowing to-do list. However, recognizing the transformative power of these connections is crucial, and practical strategies can help prioritize relationships amid the myriad demands of the profession. Rather than perceiving it as extra work, it's essential to understand that relationship building is the work itself.

To shift the mindset around relationship building, consider it an integral part of teaching. The connections forged with students significantly impact their learning experience, motivation, and overall well-being. Recognizing this intrinsic value elevates relationship building to a priority. While relationship building does take time, integrating practices into existing routines can make it more manageable. Brief check-ins with students at the beginning or end of class, even if momentary, can create a sense of connection. Seeking support and collaboration from colleagues can also be beneficial. By collectively valuing and prioritizing relationships, the teaching community contributes to a culture where this essential aspect of education is seen as a shared commitment rather than an additional burden.

Resistance and Skepticism

Navigating resistance and skepticism, whether from teachers, students, or leaders, demands a nuanced and empathetic approach.

Teachers

Addressing teachers skeptical about the transformative power of relationships requires recognition that skepticism often arises from past experiences, systemic challenges, and the pressures of the education system. Establishing open dialogue by acknowledging these factors lays the groundwork for understanding. Encourage teachers to share their reservations, fostering an environment where their voices are heard and valued. This validation not only acknowledges their experiences but also provides a nuanced understanding of perceived barriers.

Teachers who recognize the transformative power of relationships can play a pivotal role in helping skeptical peers understand and embrace this perspective. Act as a resource by sharing personal experiences showcasing the positive impact of meaningful connections on your teaching journey. Offer collaborative lesson planning or activities incorporating relationship-building strategies to allow skeptics to witness the positive impact firsthand. Collaboration on projects highlighting the collective benefits of prioritizing student-teacher relationships within the school community is valuable.

Create informal spaces for dialogue where teachers can openly discuss concerns. Initiate book clubs or discussion groups focused on literature emphasizing the importance of relationships in education. Fostering a supportive community within the staff allows teachers to share insights, strategies, and success stories, gradually influencing skeptics. Encourage continuous learning through workshops or sessions led by educators who successfully navigated similar challenges. Active participation shapes a school culture valuing the relational aspect of education.

Students

Assisting students who may have lost trust in teachers demands an empathetic and sensitive approach. Create a safe space for them to share experiences and feelings without judgment. Demonstrating genuine care involves a sincere interest in their overall well-being. Incorporate personal check-ins or discussions about their interests and aspirations to show that you value them as individuals. Implementing restorative practices provides structured opportunities for reflection, expression, and meaningful conversations.

Encourage students to actively shape the classroom community by seeking their input on norms and expectations. This participatory approach fosters a sense of ownership and agency, contributing to trust rebuilding. Consistency is crucial; be reliable in actions and commitments, consistently demonstrating support. Follow through on promises related to academic support, feedback, or additional resources. Maintaining a consistent and caring presence rebuilds trust gradually, creating an environment where students feel valued, understood, and supported.

Leaders

When dealing with data-focused leaders, integrate relationship-building strategies with evidence-based educational practices. Create data narratives linking positive academic outcomes to strong teacher-student relationships. Share instances where improved relationships resulted in noticeable improvements. Align relationship-building language with educational goals to bridge the gap between data priorities and interpersonal connections.

Demonstrate a commitment to understanding and navigating the data-driven landscape. Contribute constructively to discussions by showcasing the symbiotic relationship between robust relationships and academic achievement. Position relationship-building not as a diversion but as a complementary and essential component for sustainable educational success. This proactive approach fosters a culture of mutual understanding and collaboration between teachers and data-focused leaders.

Addressing resistance or skepticism necessitates patience, empathy, and dedication to building a shared vision prioritizing the holistic development of students. Actively involve stakeholders, acknowledge concerns, and consistently demonstrate the positive impact of relationship-building practices to create a more receptive and collaborative educational environment.

Conclusion

Teacher-student relationships are not just a facet of education; they are the heart of it.

In the exploration of the intricate necessities of teacher-student relationships, Samantha's journey serves as a poignant illustration of the transformative power embedded within these connections. Throughout my research and experience, several key takeaways emerge, underscoring the profound impact of genuine, empathetic, and supportive teacher-student relationships on the educational landscape.

Key Takeaways

Empathy as a Catalyst for Growth:

Samantha's experience emphasizes the pivotal role of empathy in a student's educational journey. To Samantha, teachers who demonstrated a caring and empathetic approach stood out, creating an environment where students felt valued, understood, and supported. This quality, Samantha contends, is not just a soft skill but a transformative force that propels students toward academic success and personal growth. Not only did it improve feelings of value and well being in the classroom, but it also worked to chip away at past trauma and led to robust academic success. This serves to underscore an experience that encapsulates the resilience and transformative potential ignited by supportive teacher-student relationships. The contrast between professors who adhered to rigid systems and those who adopted hands-on, interactive approaches becomes a testament to the critical role educators play in students' ability to overcome obstacles. Samantha also names for us the importance of accountability ("love and care") to this recipe.

Life Beyond Academics

Beyond the academic realm, Samantha's reflections extend to the lasting influence of teacher-student relationships on her professional life. The skills cultivated through supportive interactions—such as resilience, a positive mindset, and the ability to embrace challenges—proved instrumental in navigating the complexities of the working world. The notion that education extends far beyond the classroom walls becomes evident, with teachers serving as architects of not only academic success but also lifelong skills that shape individuals in various aspects of their lives. Life after school is often, of course, heavily dependent on what we know and have learned in our coursework. I contend that it is also *even more so dependent* on what we have learned about failure, self love, forgiveness, and relationship building.

Reinforcing the Potential for Transformative Change:

The collective narrative articulated in this exploration resoundingly reinforces the potential for transformative change through meaningful relationships in education at all levels. It accentuates that these connections are not ancillary to the educational process but are *integral to its very core.* The ripple effect of empathetic and supportive teacher-student relationships extends beyond individual academic achievements, fostering a sense of belonging, resilience, and positive identity within the school community. From there is created a sort of "pay it forward" mentality that has the potential to impact generations of young people both inside and outside of school system.

Encouraging Adaptation and Application:

As we conclude this exploration, the spotlight shifts to the readers—educators, administrators, and anyone invested in the educational sphere. The richness of Samantha's journey beckons readers to adapt and apply the principles elucidated within their own contexts. The call is for a collective acknowledgment of the potential each person holds to contribute to transformative change through intentional relationship-building. Educators are encouraged to embrace empathy as a guiding force, recognizing that the ability to understand and connect with students on a personal level is not a luxury but a necessity. The stories shared by Samantha underscore that the impact of a caring teacher reaches far beyond the confines of the academic curriculum. In the face of challenges, educators are called upon to nurture resilience by creating environments that support students emotionally and academically. The example of Samantha's triumph over a difficult math course illuminates the significance of educators in fostering a growth mindset and instilling in students the belief that setbacks are not insurmountable hurdles, but instead, a normal and necessary part of life. There are and have been many commentaries on this idea for centuries, but to put it simply: *Failure is a necessary step towards authentic and consistent success.*

The Last Word

In essence, the transformative power of relationships in education emerges as a shared commitment. It is a commitment to creating learning environments where every student feels seen, heard, and valued. It is a commitment to fostering not only academic success but also the development of skills and attitudes that equip individuals for the challenges of life beyond school. As we close this exploration, the resonating message is clear: *teacher-student relationships are not just a facet of education; they are the heart of it.* The potential for transformative change lies within the hands of educators who recognize and harness the power of these connections, shaping not only the educational journey but the very fabric of our society. The call is for all stakeholders in education to unite in this shared commitment, building environments where empathy, support, and transformative growth are at the forefront of the educational narrative.

Made in the USA
Las Vegas, NV
26 January 2024

84948115R00030